Sisters in Another Life

prose by

Talia Weisz

Finishing Line Press
Georgetown, Kentucky

Sisters in Another Life

ACKNOWLEDGMENTS

"Treehuggers" was published in Hermeneutic Chaos Journal (March 2016, Issue #13)

I would like to thank the Crown Heights Writers Society for their intelligent and invaluable feedback.

My deepest gratitude to Gail Marlene Schwartz and John Hubbell for their love, insight, and creative midwifery.

Special thanks to Natalie Kershaw for the poem she wrote to me in our youth, and for giving me permission to quote it in "Angie."

Publisher: Leah Maines

Editor: Christen Kincaid

Cover Art: Nicole St. Michel

Author Photo: John Hubbell

Cover Design: Elizabeth Maines McCleavy

Printed in the USA on acid-free paper.
Order online: www.finishinglinepress.com
also available on amazon.com

Author inquiries and mail orders:
Finishing Line Press
P. O. Box 1626
Georgetown, Kentucky 40324
U. S. A.

Table of Contents

For John and Gail

Feral Girls

<u>Hanson, circa 1997</u>

The first time I saw you three on MTV, I mistook you for girls: flat-chested, exuberant girls in baggy jeans and no makeup, bounding across the beach like cocker spaniels on the loose. Leaping through waves, tumbling in the sand, ruddy and exotic: feral girls who had never learned to hate themselves like the rest of us.

<u>Caroline</u>

We both have our sob stories. Kyle Bachman punching me in the gut in second grade, laughing as I crumpled like a paper bag. Those girls who told you to close your eyes and hold out your hands for a surprise, then poured yogurt on your head—spoiled yogurt, lumpy and mixed with pencil shavings, all of it dripping down your hair and onto your school cardigan.

And here we are at twelve: Hunkered down at our desks every afternoon until dark, we pull off straight A's, each one seeming like a fluke, like something we don't deserve. "I like it," you say of your grim regimen—the dinners you scarf down alone to save time, the frantic nights spent memorizing flash cards. I pretend not to notice your ruined fingertips, the way you pick at them absently, opening the skin. When I ask to borrow your biology notes, you look me square in the eyes and enunciate every word: "If you lose them, I will kill you. If you dirty them, I will kill you."

<u>Lena</u>

In the shower, you tell me I look weird, and I'm confused. You point at my naked chest. "It's weird you have boobs." We've been showering together for years—sculpting foamy shampoo hairdos, comparing bellybuttons and birthmarks.

"It's weird you *don't*," is all I can think to retort. Your boobs, if you can call them that, are little nubs, dog teats. We are thirteen. The following week, I insist we shower in separate stalls.

"*Why*?" you protest.

"What're you, a pervert?"

You sulk off, but later creep back to peek at me through the wet curtain. "Hey!" I splutter, the soap in my eyes blurring you—your naked butt a streak of white, your shrill hyena laugh echoing off the tile walls.

Angie

We aren't angry at each other, we just tussle for fun. Twist each others' arms, give Chinese sunburns, our nails leaving welts in the other's flesh. "You bitch," we say, briefly sobered by our wounds. "Look what you did." It passes the time. Like the notes we scribble in the margins of my textbook:
HI!
get away from me
You're so nice. Fuck you.
don't take this personally but shut up
I'm so insulted. so wuz up?
not much wuz ↑ with u?
Nothing. Life Sucks.
so why don't u just lay in your rut + die
OK!!

Tamara
We are fourteen when you kiss me on the neck in the middle of Sam's Records—playfully, without warning; a sly, nimble peck that

sends me spinning too high to a place with no air. You laugh. "Now everyone's gonna think we're lesbians," you deadpan, and I pray you can't hear the gulls thrashing in my chest.

In your room, I sit with my knees folded up like an origami shield, and you ask me if I am cold. At your dinner table, I try not to look at you too much—your dimpled cheeks, the shaggy silk of your hair, your perfect teeth. You burn through my peripheral vision. I fumble with my cutlery, knock over my glass, spill grape juice on the tablecloth, jump up in alarm, my chair clattering to the floor.

"Whoa," you giggle. "Chillax."

"It'll come right out with bleach, love," your mother says as I dab stupidly at the purple Rorschach stain—garish, obscene, like a secretion from my own body.

Eloise

You are three-and-a-half and pronounce your C's like T's, and sleep in nothing but a diaper. "Give titty a tiss," you say, holding your Hello Kitty doll up to my face, and I obey—undone by your puppyish warmth and earnest china doll stare. "Mama says you have dots because you're growing up." You touch my face, reading the acne bumps like delicate braille, your fingers so gentle that I forget to be ashamed.

Treehuggers

This is how I find you: scraping greenish fur off a slice of bread, pushing the powdery flakes to one side of your plate, opening a crusty jar of marmalade. "Hey Sophie," I say, trying to sound casual. "How old is that bread?"

You take a bite and chew thoughtfully. "It's actually not so bad."

"You don't have to eat that," Angie tells you, and reaches for her wallet. "Go get some real food."

"This is real food," you say with your mouth full, waving away her five dollar bill.

＊

You wear garlands of fake flowers in your hair, Mardi Gras beads, rainbow knee socks, and you remind me of Frida Kahlo—that heart-shaped face, that wisp of a unibrow. When people ask you where you're from, you smile breezily: "Oh, I'm not really from anywhere." I am seventeen and you are eighteen, and I follow you around like a golden retriever. When people ask us if we are sisters, you squeeze my hand: "Yes, in another life." I start wearing your cast-off sweaters and vests, your costume pearls and sashes. You like to dress me up, embellish me. "There," you say, pinning a silk daisy in my hair. You step back to appraise me, like I'm a Christmas tree you've just crowned with a star.

＊

We wander downtown Montreal. Hands clasped, hairy legs swinging in unison, we amble up side streets, in and out of shops. "Mmm," you say, uncapping a vial of perfume and inhaling deeply. "I love musk. It reminds me of old churches. Here." You hold the bottle under my nose, and I breathe in, eyes closed, wanting to be transported to Venice or Budapest. When you stop to hug a tree,

I hug it too. "So beautiful," you sigh, and I sigh too, and press my cheek against the rough, peeling bark, wanting to feel what you feel in all my pores.

*

People come and go from your apartment at all hours, sometimes sleeping on the floor for weeks. We draw with colored chalk on the walls, finger-paint with our toes, play in a bath of cooked spaghetti. "Let's write a song," you say, reaching for your beat-up guitar with the missing string, and we sing without words, my voice someone else's, free as a kite relinquished to the sky. In your kitchen, we build a sculpture from the moldy remains of food—flaccid carrots and rubbery apple cores, a rotting moss-covered forest. "Isn't mold pretty," you say, "when you really look at it?" I have never really looked: all those textures and hues, abstract art born of itself.

*

You say you are a fluff of dandelion seed, that you travel on the wind. "Where will you go?" I ask, secretly hoping you'll stay. I want to keep you like a lightning bug in a jar.

Angie

<u>Neighbors</u>

Arriving home from the grocery store, we find him on the front stoop of our new apartment: hunched over a book, lanky as a sunflower. He unfurls to smile at us as we trudge up the walkway with our bags, and I try not to rush things in my mind—the awkward courtship and first kiss, the dizzying romance fast-forwarding to a vicious custody battle over the dog. By the time I register the details of his face—smooth and wan with hooded, sleepy eyes—I can barely look at him; already, there is too much history between us.

"You girls just move in?" he asks.

"Yeah," you answer for both of us. You're not shy with boys you consider a waste of time, boys who sit around in their pajamas at three in the afternoon. Following you past him through the door, through the current of his gaze, I keep my eyes on your back, the straps of your tank top digging into your burly shoulders.

*

Our apartment is cramped, in the basement, with dirt-stained windows boasting views of pedestrians' feet. There is no living room, just an alcove kitchen and a narrow hall separating our tiny bedrooms. We've made rules for ourselves: Buy everything on sale, split the grocery bills in half, be discreet about our sex lives. Not that we have them. At twenty-two, you've been on so many first dates that I can't keep your stories straight. "No," you have to correct me, "Matt was the one with borderline personality disorder. Mike was the one who got diarrhea." We laugh at these boys, so haplessly eager, so clumsy. You rarely give them a second chance.

"In ten years," you propose, "if we're both still single, let's be platonic life partners. We can buy a house and adopt a kid."

"Sure," I say half-heartedly, and you bristle.

"What, you have a better plan?"

*

I wake to the sound of wild dogs. Except it's not dogs, but a boy and girl shouting at each other over our heads in muffled gibberish. Stumbling out of my bedroom into the blinding light of the kitchen, I find you with our broom. "What are you doing?" I croak.

"What does it *look* like I'm doing?" You raise the broom handle-first and rap sharply on the ceiling.

"I don't think they can hear you."

You bang some more, then throw down the broom and storm past me. I trail after you out of our apartment and up the stairs, and now here we are at their door and you are pounding on it like the Gestapo.

Silence.

"Let's go," I whisper, but the door has opened and we're face to face with a girl: tall, strapping, all muscle and jawbone, cleavage bursting out of her tube top, her gaze steady as a cat's.

"Yeah?" She fixes us with her stare, and then *he* saunters up behind her—stubble-faced, in the same plaid bottoms he had on yesterday, a miniature poodle struggling in his arms. She whirls around. "Put George down!"

He blinks at us. "How you girls doin'?"

"Put him *down*! He hates when you hold him."

"Hey Meena, have you met our new neighbors?"

"You're a prick." The dog is writhing and kicking, trying to wriggle free. "Let him go!" She lunges at him and they tussle. He is laughing. The dog leaps from his grasp and escapes into the apartment, his nails clickety-clacking like tiny hooves.

He grins blearily at us. "See how scared he is of Meena?" She pushes past him into the apartment and re-emerges with a beaded purse on one arm, George tucked under the other, his paws dangling obediently, her flip-flops slapping the floor as she marches off down the hall. "Where you going?" he calls to the back of her head.

"Fuck you." The front door slams, and the smile melts off his face.

*

That night I dream that you and I are having sex, or trying to. Our nakedness is shocking, vaguely incestuous. Whose idea was this? We are like two bumbling bears. Inept, lethargic, we fumble with no pleasure.

*

In the morning, I find you in your room arranging your pint-size closet. "That's pretty," I say from the doorway, watching you smooth the creases of a satin blouse.

"It's a six," you shrug "I thought buying it would motivate me to lose ten pounds." Like me, you are still in your PJs, hair greasy, boobs sagging braless under a threadbare t-shirt. The dream has left me feeling clammy and a little nauseous. I watch you fold a pair of stonewashed jeans, the ones you have to suck in your stomach to zip; the assorted garments you've bought for some future version of you.

"Last night was fucked up," I say.

"Yeah," you reply without looking up. Turning back to the closet, you start humming to yourself, a tune I don't recognize. Even when we were kids, I could never tell what you were thinking. Parked in your den like stumps of petrified wood, we sat mute, blasting the TV over the crescendo of your parents' fights—your parents, who looked nothing like the couple framed on the wall: flushed and dreamy-eyed, probably stoned, her head leaning on his shoulder, like their future belonged to someone else entirely.

Parting Gifts

The summer we turn twenty five, you move to the West Coast and I move to the States. You go by car with your bearded dumpster-diving boyfriend, a rabbit named Pickles, and a trailer hooked precariously to the back of your Honda Civic. I go by plane with a suitcase full of books and not much else, to a scruffy rental studio with stained carpets and furniture left over from the last tenant: a rickety desk, a pair of mismatched drawers, a mattress on a bed-frame made of planks. Alone for the first time, I can't sleep. Staring up into the liquid darkness, I can't feel where it ends and where I begin. It flows through me, my body a translucent membrane. Maybe I don't exist. I propel myself, a jellyfish swimming through molasses, towards the tepid light of the window, to the wall where I've hung my parting gifts. From Sam, a drawing of me as a bird, crude and bespectacled, flying from a nest of glued-on feathers. From Gretchen, a banner embroidered with stars. *I love you Fiona, follow your path of dreams.* From Jen, a watercolor portrait of me, shaman-like, head alight with a crown of dazzling flames. And from you, a typed poem, bare as my skeleton:

dear fiona
you are a good person
and the sweat that comes out of your pores is blessed with 'good'

and we're each as twisted as our intestines
and our intestines are pretty twisted
and some ancient asian guy said that life is pain.

and I say "hey asian guy, moron, how will that encourage me to want
to stay alive?"

but you know the saying—"asian guys have it all figured out."
it's hard to be, and it's hard to not be.
and the limbo, which is the tug between being and not being
is actually the definition of what it means 'to be.'

Reunion

Xavier won't stop screaming, so you buy him ice cream at the dingy hospital café. "Here," you say flatly, peeling the top off the little gelato cup, and he grabs it out of your hand. He eats ferociously, sucking air through his nose, the spoon clamped in his fist, chocolate dribbling down his shirt. "No!" he snarls when you try to introduce me to him. "*No* Fiona!" He swats the air like I'm a stubborn fly. He is dark-haired like you, with a froth of curls. He doesn't know that I've spent his whole life waiting to meet him; not quite believing he is real.

"So," I say as you wheel his stroller through the sliding doors, into the blazing sun. "I guess you have a kid." Xavier is face-down, lapping ice cream off the stroller tray.

"Ta-da," you deadpan. "At least I managed to accomplish something." You: dapper in men's pleated slacks, a plaid shirt and suspenders, hair styled in a droll, lopsided faux hawk. In the five years since I last saw you in person, I've been tracking your metamorphosis—remotely, a mute spectator of your life, like a bug-eyed fish peering through the windows of a submarine.

"Let's sit here," you say, leading the way through a manicured courtyard, past a clique of smoking nurses, to a narrow patch of shade. You are visiting your mother for the first time since you left.

"How's she doing?" I ask as we sprawl out in the grass. You kick off your loafers and pull off your socks, and I'm startled to see your wide, callused feet. *Hooves*, your mother called them when we were young, making you hate them. You never went barefoot in public.

"My mother is my mother." You shoot a wry glance at your son who is nodding off in the stroller, head lolling, his gooey hand clutching the empty gelato cup. "By the way, I have to take her to her physio at three. Sorry to cut things short."

"Well, how are *you?*" Already we've wasted so much time. "Give me the cliff notes version."

"There's not much you don't know."

True, it's all on Facebook—your succession of girlfriends and menial jobs, your eccentric roommates, your crusade of self-love. Your status: *becoming the ugly duckling I always was*. In photo after photo, you pose in screaming bowties, polka dot sweater vests, gold Tootsie glasses. The old you appears once: in gaudy lipstick, flesh bulging against the seams of her skin-tight, polyester blouse. *Who's that sad femme from 2006? It's me bytches*. I'm beside her in that picture, a disembodied arm, an appendage.

"How's life in Brooklyn?" you ask. "Are you still with what's-his-name?"

"Tim. One day you'll have to meet him," I say.

"You like living with him?"

"Yeah." I don't know what else to say. I feel scattered, my life suddenly beyond description, like a Monet painting made of millions of tiny brushstrokes: sizzling onions, his hands beating a Latin jazz rhythm on the counter, bare legs tangled in sheets, the tap dance of rain against the windows. You glance at your watch.

"Hey," I blurt, "remember Caroline Kaminoff?"

You look at me strangely. "What about her?"

"I don't know, she just popped into my head." Her bleeding, picked-at fingertips. How we carried her to the nurse, each of us supporting her like a crutch, when she had that panic attack our senior year. "What's become of her?"

"I heard she's in med school."

"No kidding! You know that Lena Abrams is teaching English in Taiwan?"

"You've been talking to her?"

"We messaged once." Scrawny Lena, who spied on me in the locker room, who tried to pull down your pants in seventh grade and skulked around for a week with the black eye you gave her. "Tamara Burns is doing a PhD in neuroscience."

"Good for her." Your voice is prickly as a bur. My heart sinks. You roll your eyes, taking my silence for reproach. "Good for all of them, okay?" Your phone rings. "Hi Mummy." Wearily, you sit up, bits of grass stuck like confetti to your shirt. I can hear your mother through the speaker pressed to your ear, barking at you in a crackle of static. "Of course I didn't leave. I'm in the courtyard."

"Mamaaa," Xavier whines groggily, reaching out for you with sticky tentacle-hands.

"I said, the *courtyard*." Your voice is calm and measured. You look at me and mime shooting yourself in the head.

"MAAAMAAAAA!" Your little boy twists and squirms, straining against his seat belt. I go to him.

"Hi, Xavier," I say. "Hi sweetie." He falls into a deep, smoldering silence, our eyes locked for the first time. It's amazing, how much of you is expressed in him: your wide, brooding mouth, your burning stare. More than anything, I want to pick him up but I don't dare.

Cousins

two months

Thirteen, bent over my playpen cooing, you elicit my first smile—wet, gummy, my eyes shining saucers, my pudgy hands reaching to grasp your hair.

Nine

Your hair: lush waves cascading down your back, the tresses of a princess. I comb it out with my fingers, gather it up. Twisting, coiling, just to have it in my hands. In your parents' living room, you ambush me as I walk past—grabbing me by the waist, pulling me backwards into your lap, my skinny legs tangling with yours, your hair spilling into my eyes, our lungs heaving, like the bellows of an accordion, with laughter. Giddy, we jabber in silly cartoon voices, and I ham it up. I want to be an actress like you.

Eleven

Your apartment has mice, I hear your mother tell mine, that chew through your cereal boxes and leave droppings in your cutlery drawer. Climbing the dank and crumbling staircase, you have to watch for broken glass. I am in your old canopy bed, under the lace-trimmed duvet, listening to your mother rant. *Night and day she's running to auditions. And for what?*

Sixteen

You dye your hair a fiery copper. I chop mine off with the bathroom scissors. Me: pimple-faced, knobby knees, bad posture. Next to you, I am Quasimodo. I love you and can't bear to look at us side by side.

Eighteen

At your brother's wedding reception, I spot you from afar: swan-necked, your emerald dress cinched tight as a nineteenth century corset, your straightened hair a perfect sheath. Gleefully, I sneak up behind you and cover your eyes. "Hair!" you yelp, startling me, your hands flying to your head like I'm a swarm of diving bats. You spin around: your face is painted like a doll's, powdered and gleaming, your eyebrows traced on. "Please don't do that," you implore, and I recoil, wounded. Your gaze drifts past me to the mirrored wall, your hand smoothing a stray lock. "Gotta look good for the pictures."

twenty-one

Your new apartment has a uniformed doorman in the lobby. Sleek marble counters, a miniature washer/dryer. Your new boyfriend has a lean, kind face and a rumbling baritone. At your mother's birthday party I watch you dance with him—his sweep of honey-colored hair grazing your cheek, your mouth whispering in his ear—imagining myself in your place.

twenty-three

I show you off. "There she is!" I say, pausing the film to point you out in the background of a crowd scene. Your face orbits into view like a flash of sun through the clouds. "That's her! That's my cousin!" I jab my finger at the screen. My friends try to look impressed.

Thirty

Your bathroom walls are plastered with old photos of you backstage: in a leopard print dress with your summer stock cast. In a long witch's wig. At forty-three, you live alone—your fridge crammed with cartons of expired soy milk, old take-out, unopened bottles of health food store supplements. I make you apple crisp and split pea soup in the kitchen you never use. Since you gave up acting to work in an office, you've gained some weight around your face, a pillowy softness around your middle. "My babies!" you declare, showing me the ultrasound photo you keep framed on the TV set: your ovaries, a grainy, primordial landscape, speckled with black dots—your last eggs, the ghosts of children you might still have if you are lucky. You are hunting for a mate, rushing across the city after work to singles salsa parties, wine tastings, charity auctions. From the doorway, I watch you apply the layers of your mask, concealing the delicate spider lines around your mouth, the crinkled skin at the corners of your eyes— re-drawing yourself, your lips pressed together in concentration, and I want to smack the pencil out of your hand. "You don't need that," I gently protest, and you smile. "Yes, I do." *You're perfect and you always were*. I don't say it but I want to.

Dani, 1986-2010

I dreamed we were old friends—the sort who, at one time, ran squealing through the yard, plump, naked, pretending to fly. Dream-me had pictures of us: splashing each other in my plastic kiddie pool, napping in my crib, newborns entwined like a pair of eels.

In real life we met as graduate students. To spot you in the hall was to glimpse a vibrant flash, a burst of plumage, gone in a blink. Sometimes you alighted long enough to notice me. "Mm," you said once, nodding at the leftovers I was microwaving. "What kind of chicken is that?"

"I just baked it with some herbs. Want some?"

"Oh no, that's okay." You were zipping up your jacket, already veering towards the door. Always late, breathless. "I wish I had time to cook."

"You should come over for dinner." I had the strongest urge to feed you, to soothe your frazzled nerves. To sit you down on my ratty sofa, wrap an afghan around your taut, wiry frame.

You paused. "Dinner sounds great."

"How about Wednesday?"

"Oh, I don't know about this week." In the doorway, you flashed me a tight, painful smile. I still see it in my dreams, like a wall of barbed wire.

Eloise

You enter the bus from the back, and plop down in a seat diagonal from me. Your name swells inside me like a hundred violins. It has to be you. Round eyes and dimpled chin, sleek baby doll bangs—that same sweet face, but ripened, embellished: your cherub's nose pierced, your mouth a red berry. You wear a black turtleneck and scuffed combat boots—a woman, twenty years old at least. All these years, in my mind, you've been three, padding through your house in a diaper, your high-pitched voice and funny speech preserved like a recording. *Turn on the nightlight so titty won't get stared.* You are fingering the strap of your tattered book bag, gazing out the filthy window, a smile playing across your lips. Daydreaming. I shouldn't stare at you but I do. I am your fairy godmother, unbeknownst to you, conjuring a force field around your precious life.

I, who once woke up alone at 3am, Tim's side of the bed cold, convinced he had died. Who thought, *if he's dead, I will hang myself.* Who thought, *I might decay in this apartment for years.* My corpse undetected over the smells of our neighbors' cooking, my friends too steeped in their lives to call. Like that woman discovered by the bailiffs on her sofa—the flesh rotted off her bones, in front of a blaring television, surrounded by Christmas presents she'd wrapped and never sent.

You rise from your seat. The bus lurches to a halt. I hold you like a butterfly cupped in my hands. You turn towards the doors, oblivious to me. When I release you, you leave a powder residue on my skin.

Talia Weisz was born and raised in Montreal. She holds a Bachelor of Arts in Creative Writing and Anthropology from Concordia University, and a Master of Arts in Comparative Studies from The Ohio State University. Her first chapbook, *When Flying Over Water*, was published by Plan B Press in 2009. She currently lives in Brooklyn, NY, where she teaches yoga to children, attempts to knit things, and is trying to sprout an avocado pit on her windowsill.